HOW TO DRAW
WINTER THINGS

for kids

ALLI KOCH

Paige Tate & Co.

Copyright © 2024 Alli Koch
Published by Paige Tate & Co.
Paige Tate & Co. is an imprint of Blue Star Press
PO Box 8835, Bend, OR 97708
contact@bluestarpress.com
www.bluestarpress.com

All rights reserved. No part of this publication may be reproduced or transmitted in any form or by any means, electronic or mechanical, including photocopy, recording, or any information storage and retrieval system, without permission in writing from the publisher.

Written and illustrated by Alli Koch

ISBN: 9781963183092

Printed in Colombia

10 9 8 7 6 5 4 3 2 1

this book
BELONGS TO

_____

LET'S DRAW!

The nice thing about being an artist is that you can make the rules. Everyone has their own style, which is why your drawings will look different from someone else's. In this book, each project is broken down into easy-to-follow steps. My goal is to help you see the simple parts of what may seem like a hard thing to draw.

We will start with the most basic outline or guide and work our way up. You will start to see a pattern with each wintery thing we draw, starting with simple guidelines, then breaking down "C" and "S" shaped lines, and lastly erasing the unneeded lines for the finished look. Don't forget to draw your lines lightly first so it is easier to erase them. My favorite thing to say when drawing is:

If it was perfect, it would not look handmade!

I cannot wait for you to get started. Happy drawing!

TOOLS

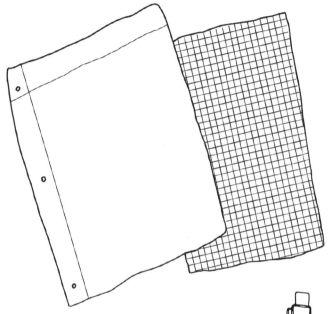

The cool thing about art is that you can use any tool you want! Yep, that's right! You are the artist, so feel free to be creative. For this book, let's keep it simple. It's easy to learn using either blank sheets of paper or grid paper.

When you are learning to draw, you really only need a pencil and a good eraser. To follow the step-by-step instructions, draw everything lightly, then go over your lines with whatever tool you would like to use. You can use different pens, markers, colored pencils, or even crayons to add details to your drawings.

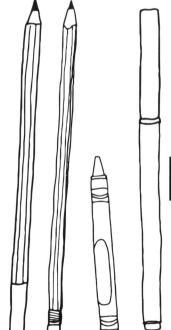

CIRCLES CAN BE TRICKY. TRY USING A PENNY OR A CIRCLE STENCIL TO HELP!

BREAK IT DOWN

Anyone can draw! If you can write your ABCs (which I am pretty sure you can do!), then you can draw everything in this book. Each project can be broken down into a bunch of "C" and "S" shaped lines. Almost anything that is round is two simple "C" shaped lines put together. An "S" shaped line is for when something has a dip or curvy line.

Most of the projects in this book are broken down into six or eight steps. What you need to draw in each step will appear as a black line; what you have already drawn will appear as gray lines. There are more than 40 winter-themed illustrations in this book for you to learn how to draw. The chapter dividers in this book are also bonus coloring pages that you can color!

WHEN IT SNOWS

SNOWMAN

The largest snowman ever made was 122 feet tall! It was created in 2008 in Bethel, Maine.

1

2

3

4

5

6

SNOWFLAKE

No two snowflakes are alike! Each snowflake has its own unique pattern.

1

2

3

4

5

6

ABOMINABLE SNOWMAN

The abominable snowman—also called the *yeti*—is a big, ape-like creature that's said to live in the Himalayas.

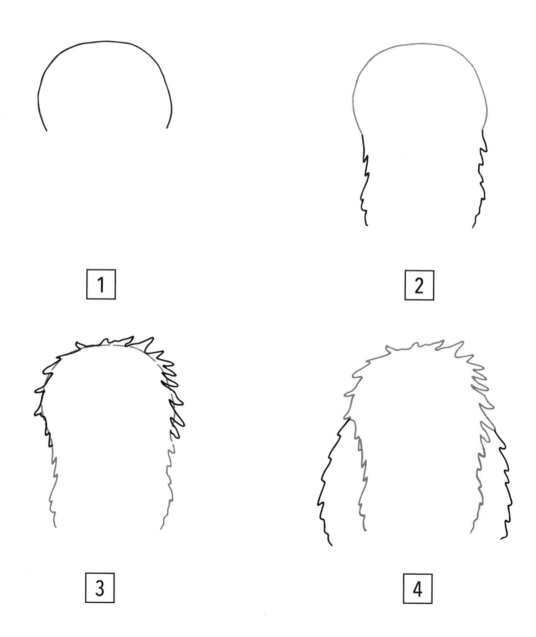

1

2

3

4

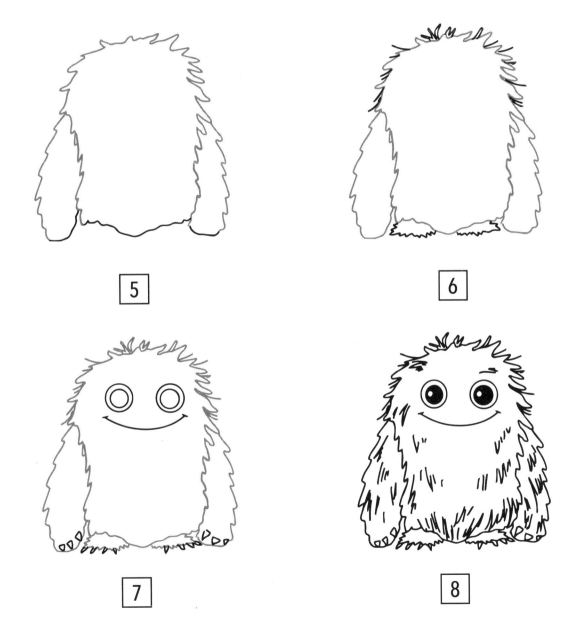

5

6

7

8

SNOW GLOBE

The world record for the most snow globes owned is 4,238!

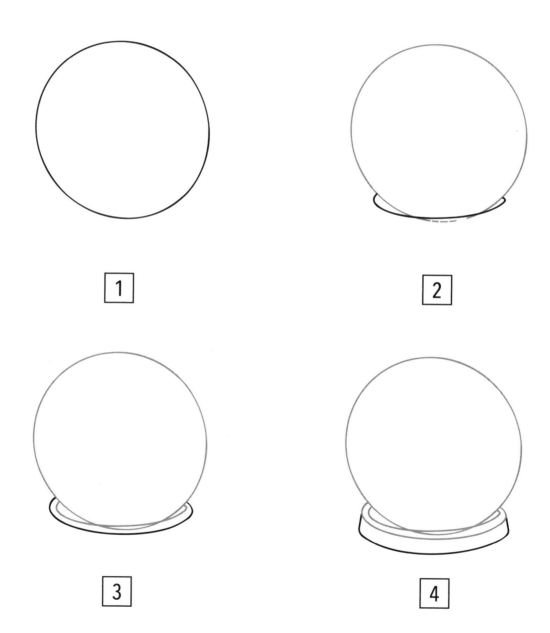

1

2

3

4

5

6

7

8

SLED

One of the world's longest sled rides is nearly 8 miles long.

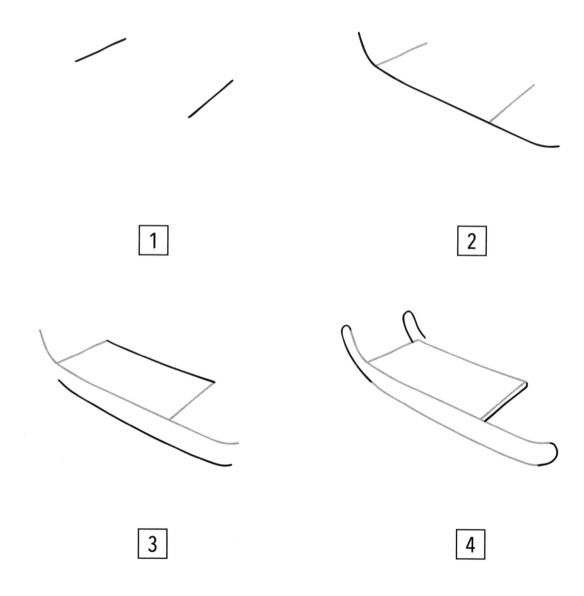

1

2

3

4

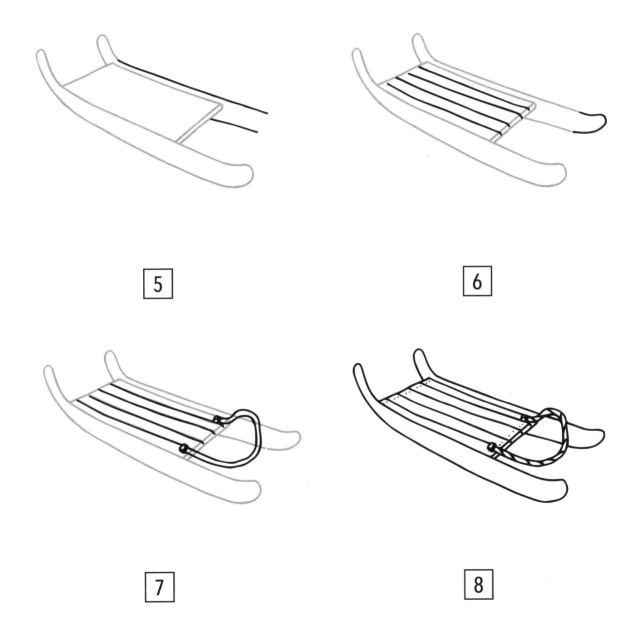

5

6

7

8

BEANIE

In Canada, beanies are called *toques*.

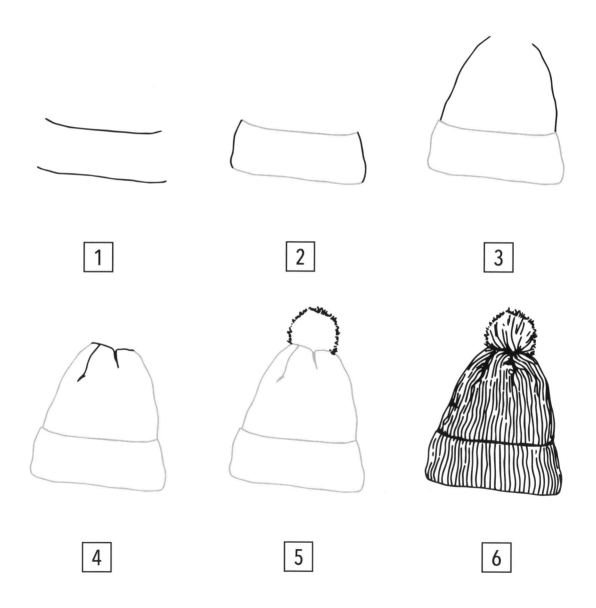

EARMUFFS

In 1873, a fifteen-year-old from Maine invented the modern-day earmuff.

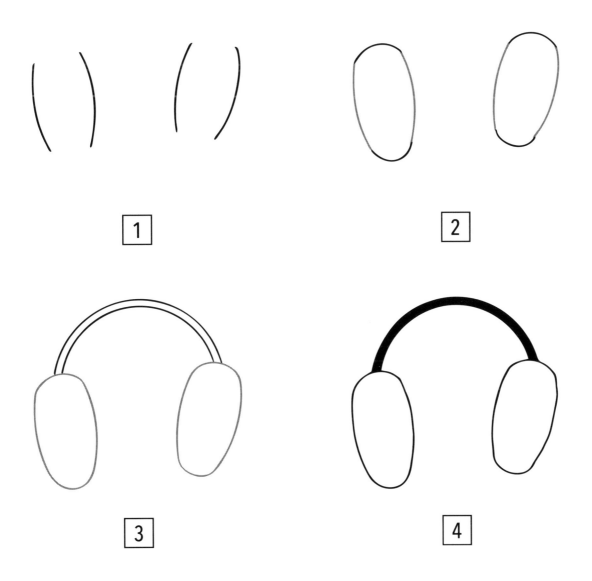

SCARF

The longest hand-woven scarf is about 3,772 feet.

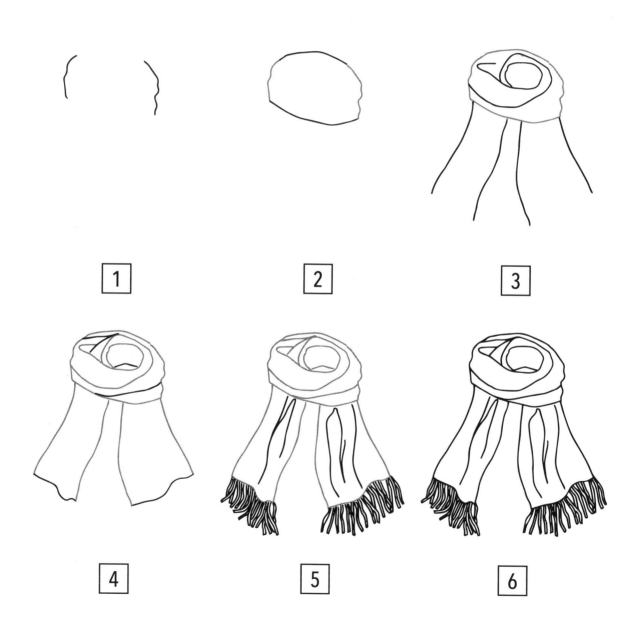

MITTENS

Mittens tend to be warmer than gloves because our fingers generate more heat when they are together.

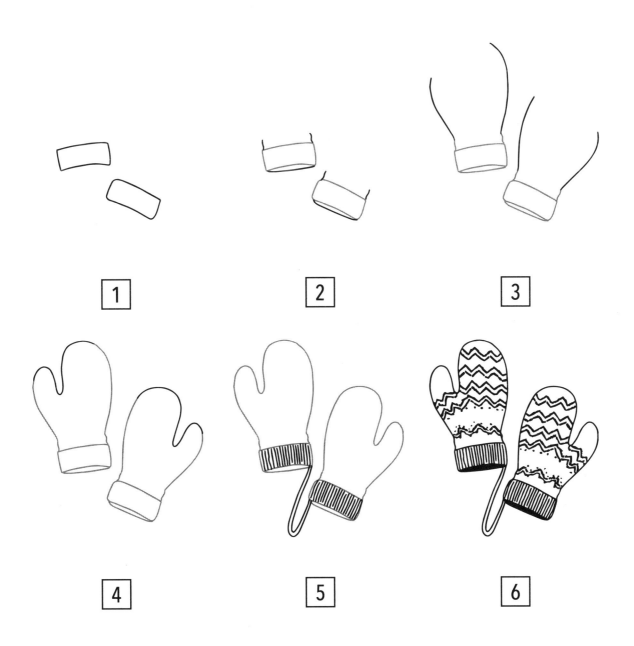

1

2

3

4

5

6

ICE SKATES

History suggests that ice skating has been around since 1000 BCE. The first ice skates were often made from oxen, elk, or reindeer bones.

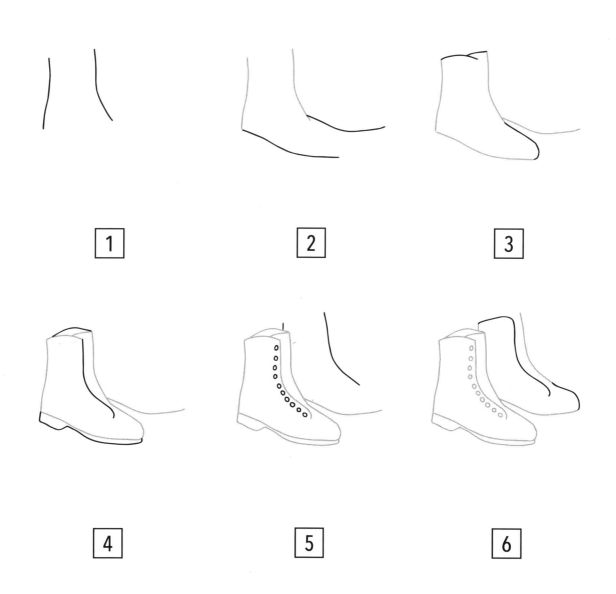

1

2

3

4

5

6

7

8

9

10

11

12

SWEATER

The largest sweater ever made was 151-feet long and 52.5-feet wide.
That's almost half the size of a football field!

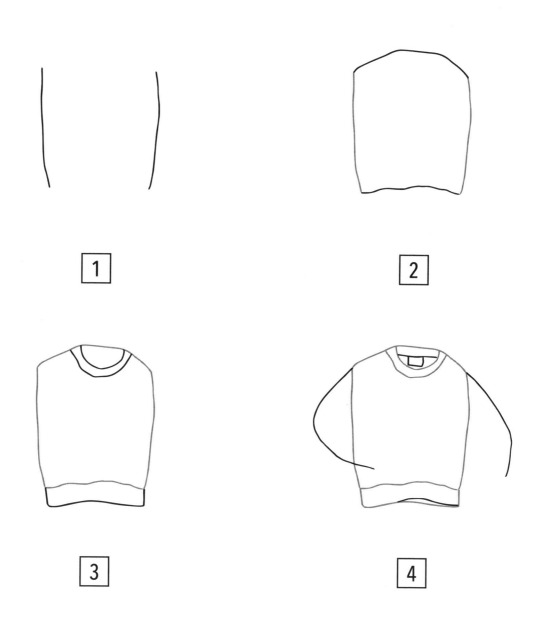

1

2

3

4

5

6

7

8

NATURE IN WINTER

POINSETTIA

Known as the flower of Christmas Eve, poinsettias are considered symbols of luck and prosperity.

1

2

3

4

5

6

7

8

MISTLETOE

Mistletoe is an evergreen plant, which means it will stay green all year long!

1

2

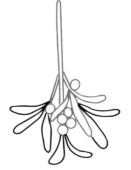

3

4

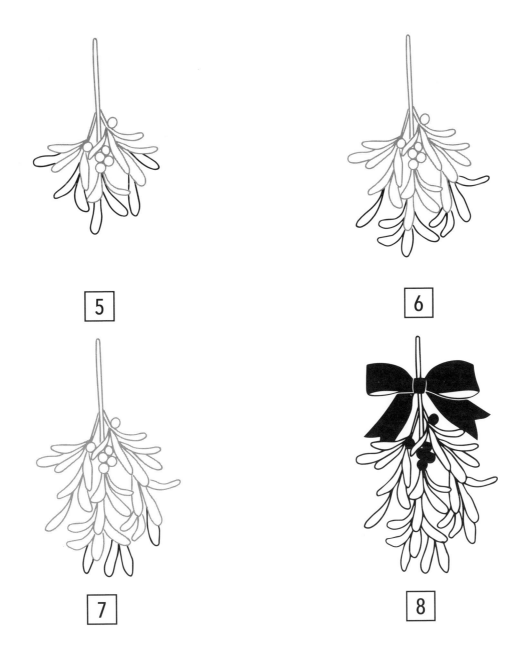

5

6

7

8

HOLLY

Holly is known for having tough, spiky leaves, which help deter animals from eating it.

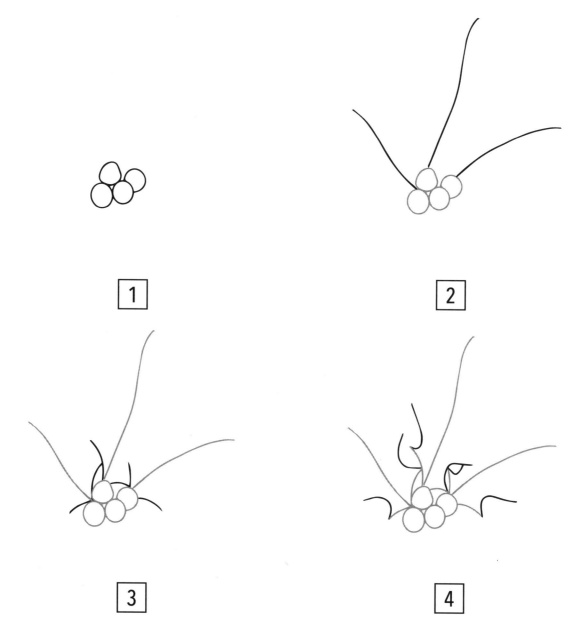

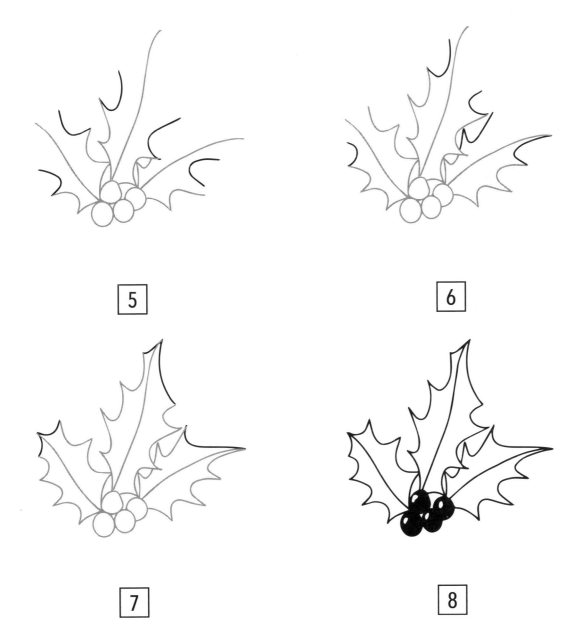

5

6

7

8

33

EVERGREEN TREE

Evergreen trees can be found on every continent except Antarctica.

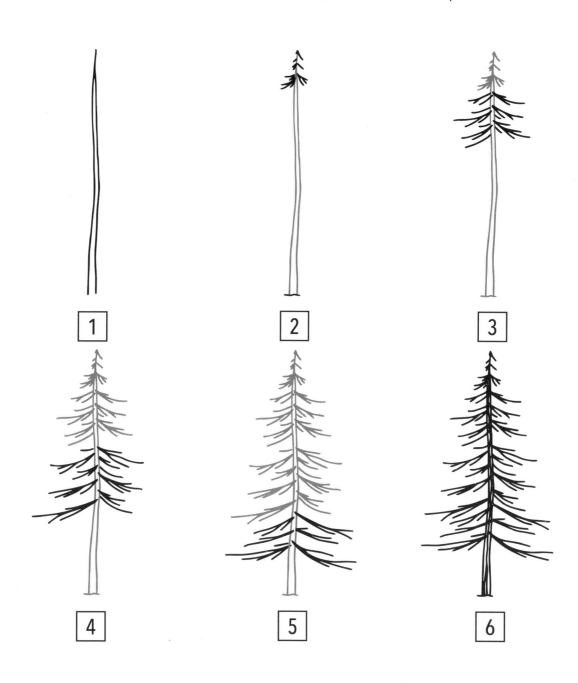

EVERGREEN TREE

More then 630 types of evergreen plants are known as *conifers*, which means they grow cones.

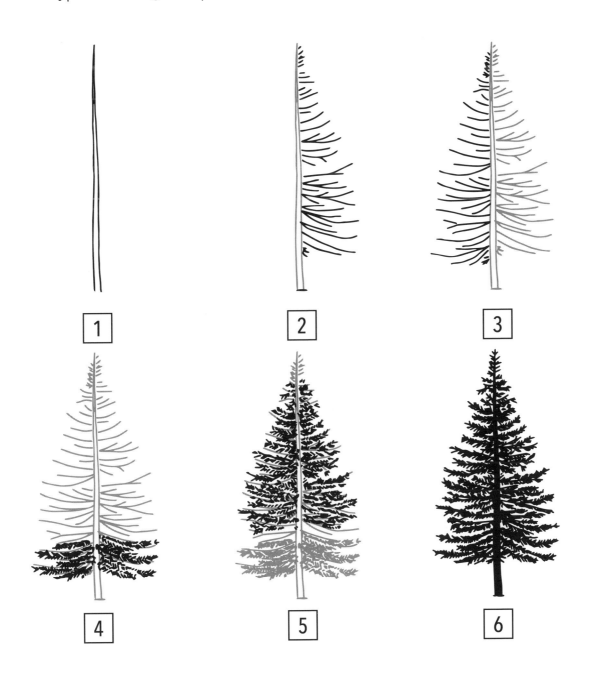

WREATH

Wreaths can be made from an assortment of flowers, twigs, berries, and leaves.
Plus, you can make mini wreaths to hang as ornaments!

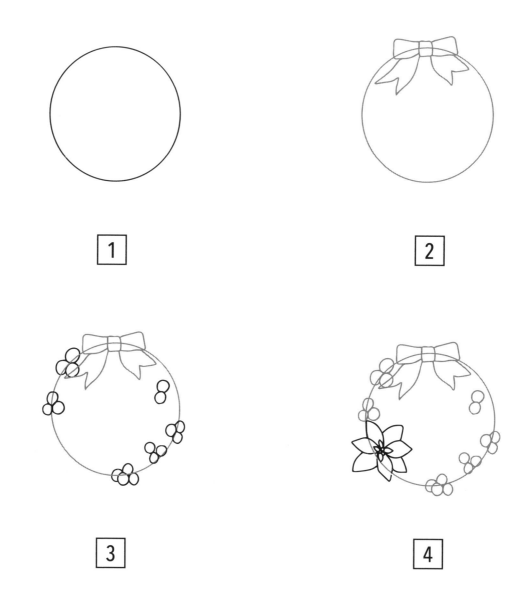

1

2

3

4

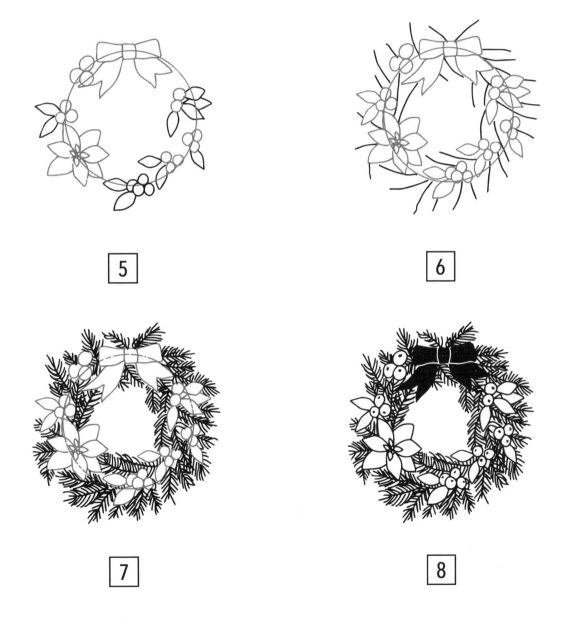

5

6

7

8

SNOWY OWL

Snowy owls have white feathers, which help them blend in with the snow during winter.

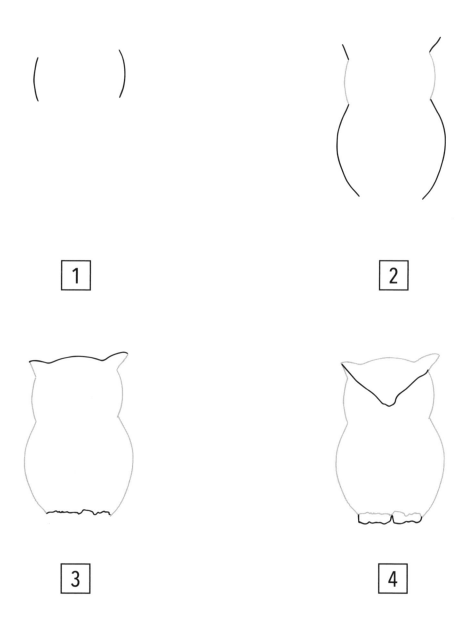

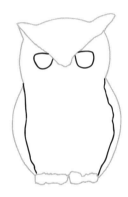

5

6

7

8

39

WINTER FOX

A fox's coat can change color each season, from snowy white in the winter to brown in the summer.

1

2

3

4

5

6

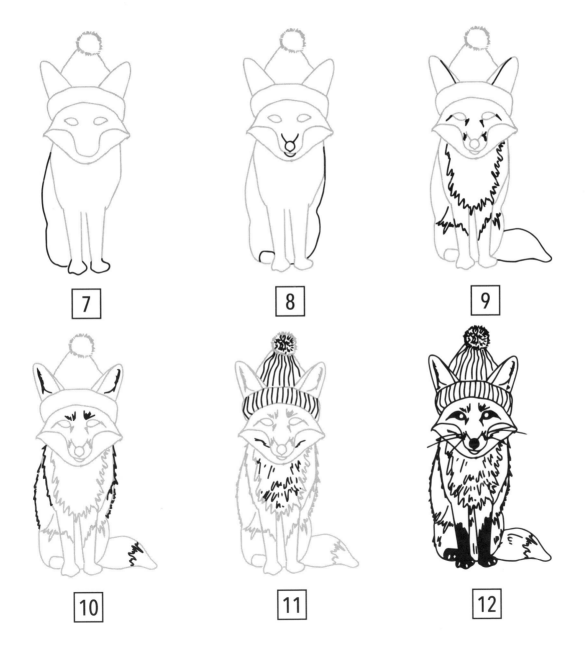

7

8

9

10

11

12

BEAR

Polar bear paws are covered with small bumps to help them grip the ice.

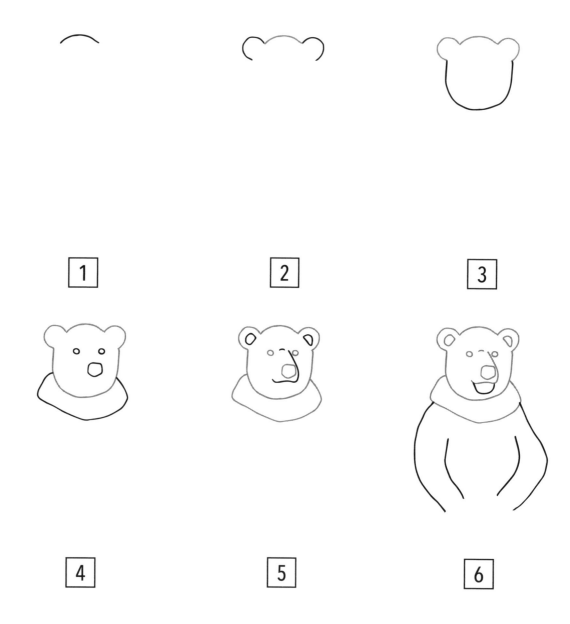

7

8

9

10

11

12

PENGUIN

Emperor penguins can hold their breath underwater for up to 27 minutes.

1

2

3

4

5

6

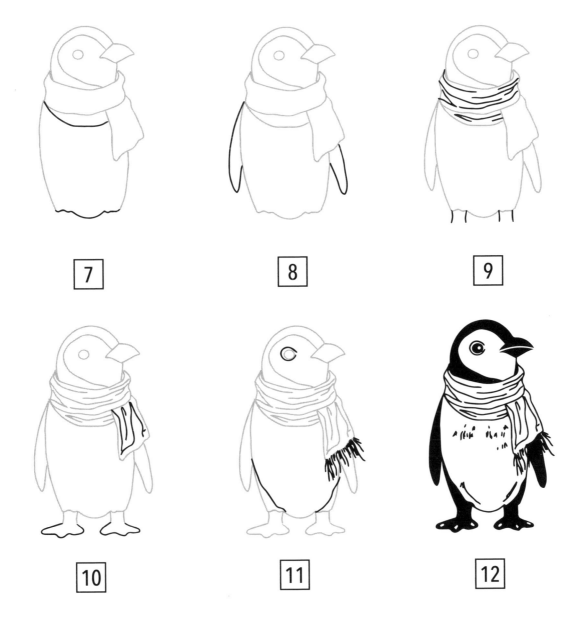

7

8

9

10

11

12

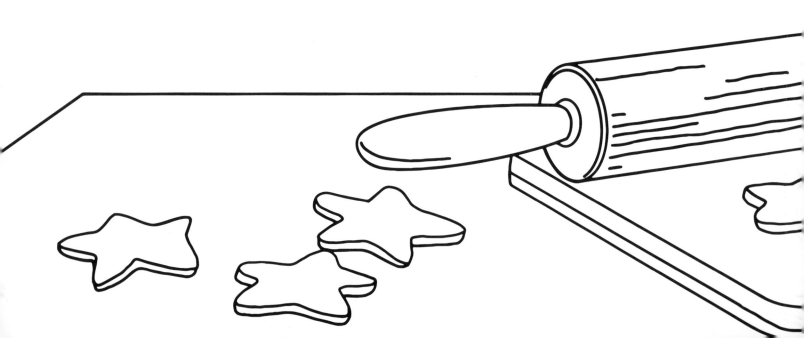

WINTER TREATS

HOT COCOA

The first iteration of hot cocoa was invented by the Mayans around 500 BC. They would combine ground-up cocoa seeds, water, cornmeal, and chili peppers.

1

2

3

4

5

6

7

8

GINGERBREAD BOY

In 2009, the IKEA store in Oslo, Norway, baked the world's largest gingerbread man.
It weighed 1,435 pounds!

GINGERBREAD GIRL

Queen Elizabeth I is credited with inventing the person-shaped gingerbread cookie. She had the cookies decorated to look like some of her most important guests!

1

2

3

4

5

6

GINGERBREAD HOUSE

National Gingerbread House Day is December 12. This would be a great day to make your own gingerbread house!

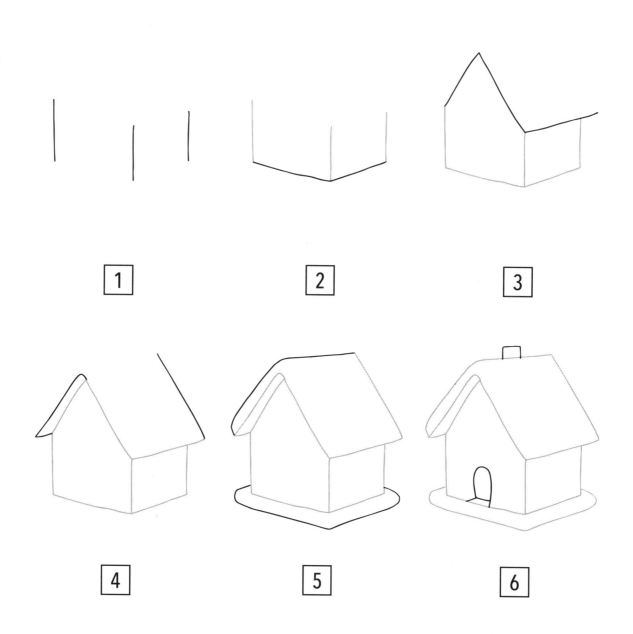

7

8

9

10

11

12

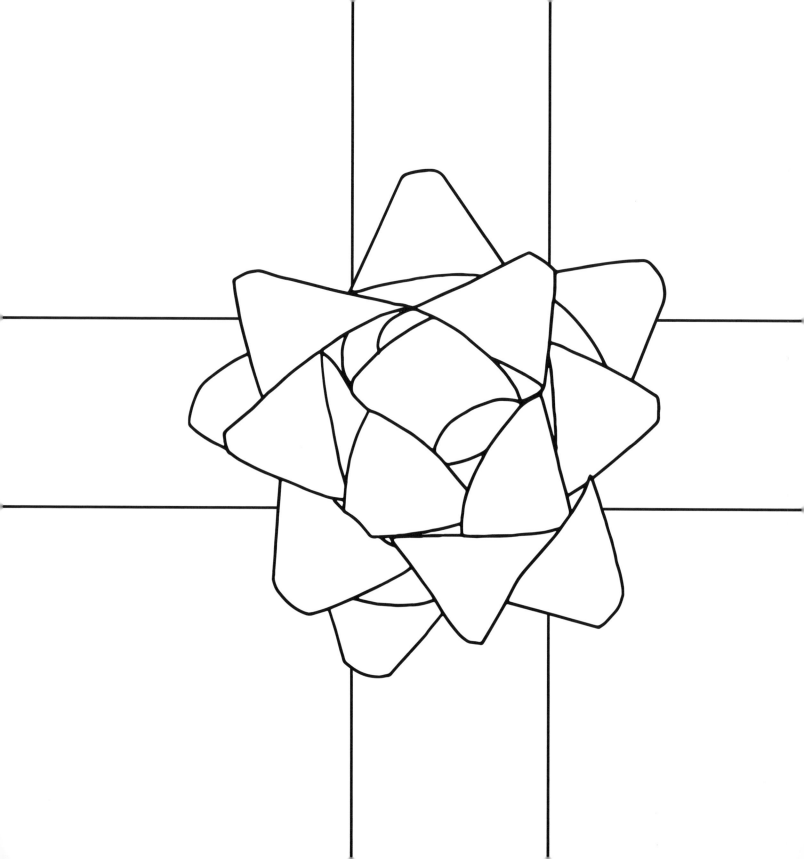

THE HOLIDAYS

CHRISTMAS TREE

According to Guinness World Records, the tallest cut Christmas tree was 221 feet tall.

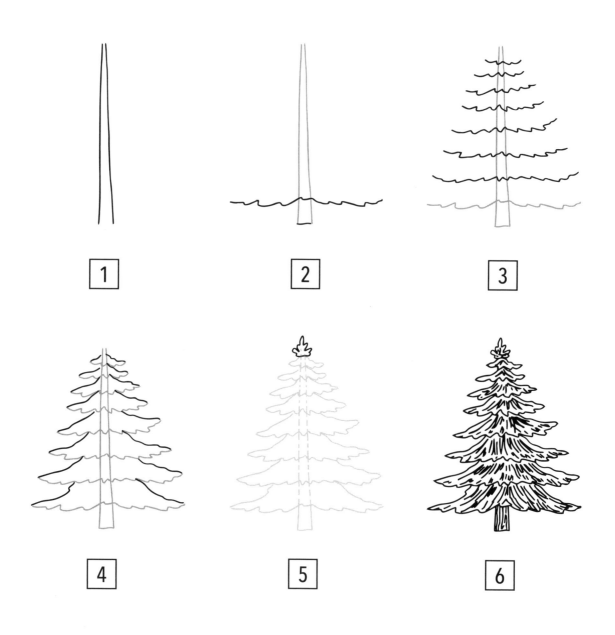

CANDY CANE

More than 1.76 billion candy canes are produced each year.

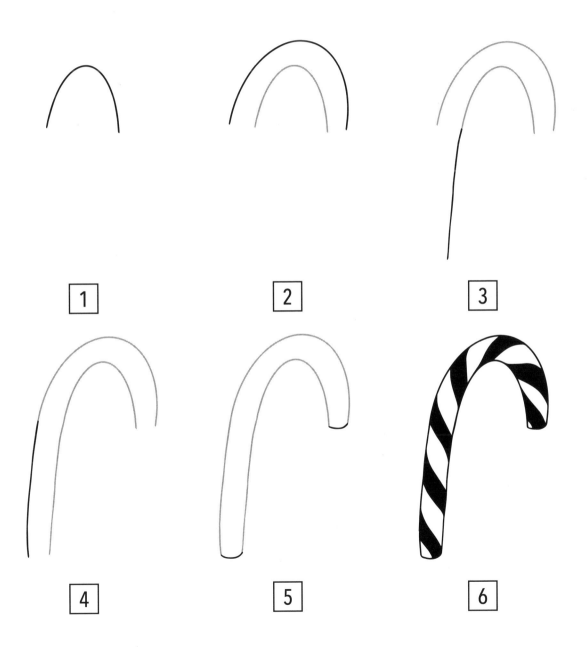

1

2

3

4

5

6

SANTA

Santa's favorite drink to pair with cookies is eggnog.

1

2

3

4

5

6

7

8

9

10

11

12

ELF

Elves work year-round to make toys for Christmas.

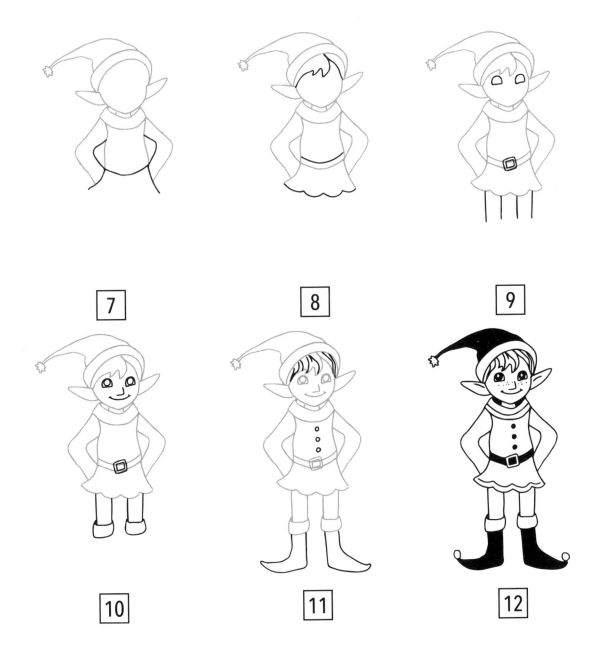

7

8

9

10

11

12

REINDEER

Santa's nine reindeer help him fly his sleigh! Can you name them all?

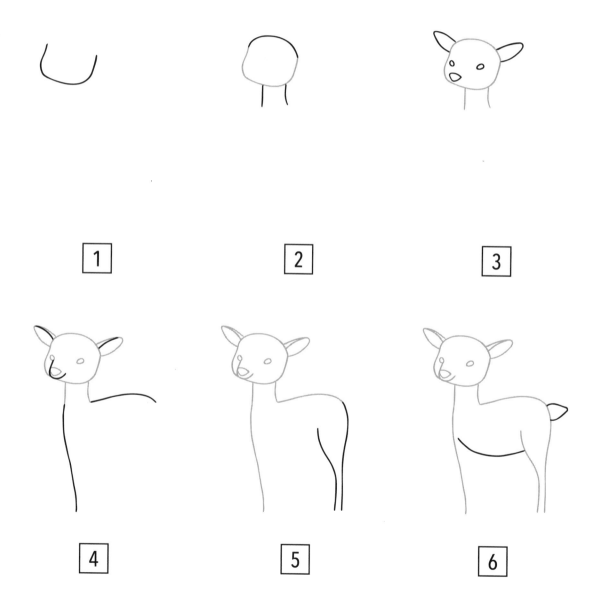

1

2

3

4

5

6

7

8

9

10

11

12

RIBBON

Among many uses, ribbons can be used to decorate wrapped presents,
Christmas trees, festive wreaths, and even the outside of your house!

PEPPERMINT

Not only is peppermint good in candy, but it makes a yummy tea, too!

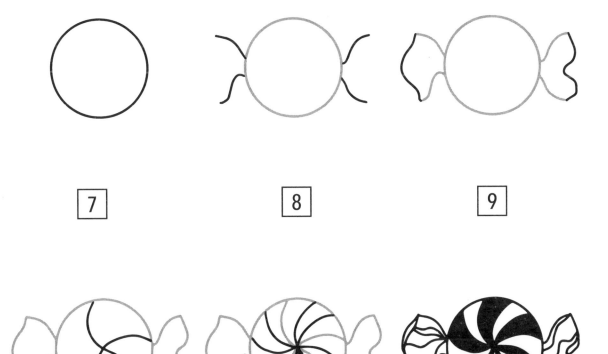

7

8

9

10

11

12

JINGLE BELLS

"Jingle Bells" was the first song broadcast from space.

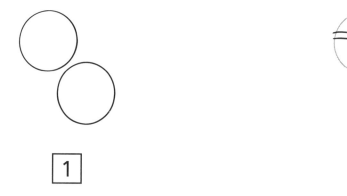

1

3

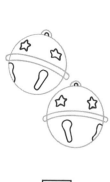

4

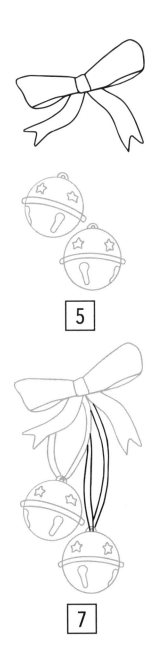

5

7

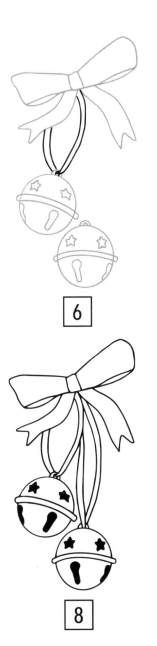

6

8

ORNAMENT

Before ornaments, people used to decorate Christmas trees with apples!

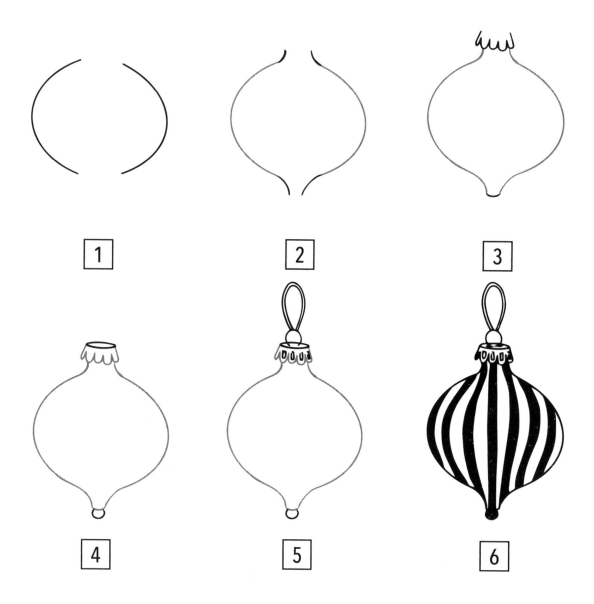

STOCKING

Stockings are a popular Christmas tradition around the world. Some traditional stocking stuffers include oranges, coins, candy, and small toys.

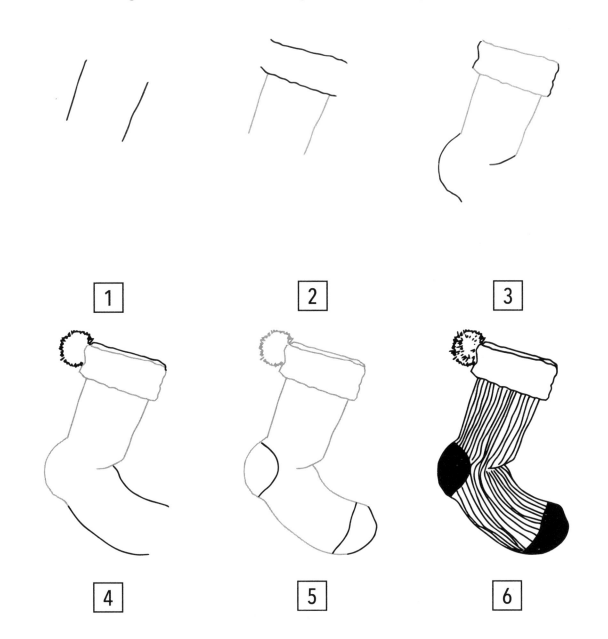

HANUKKAH MENORAH

A menorah has nine candles: eight candles represent the eight nights of Hanukkah, and the ninth candle is the "helper candle" that is used to light the others.

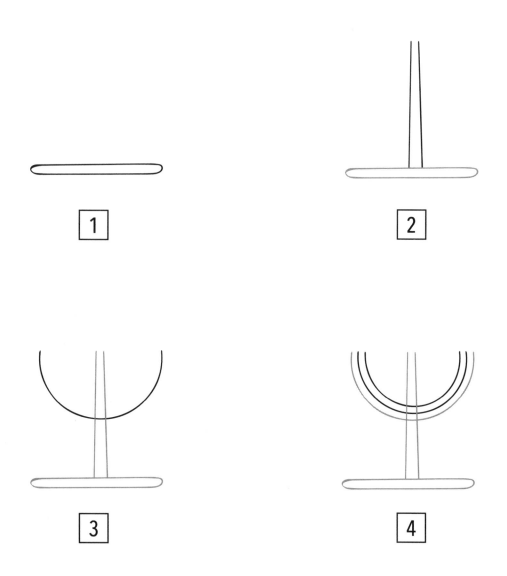

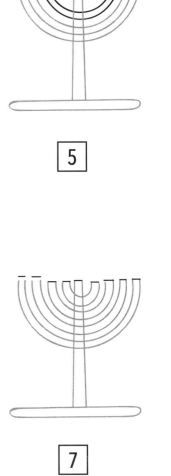

5

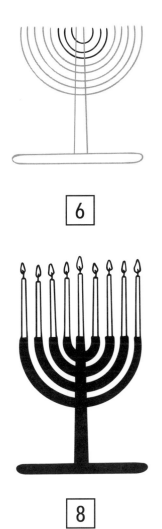

6

7

8

DREIDEL

The word *dreidel* comes from the Yiddish word for "turn."

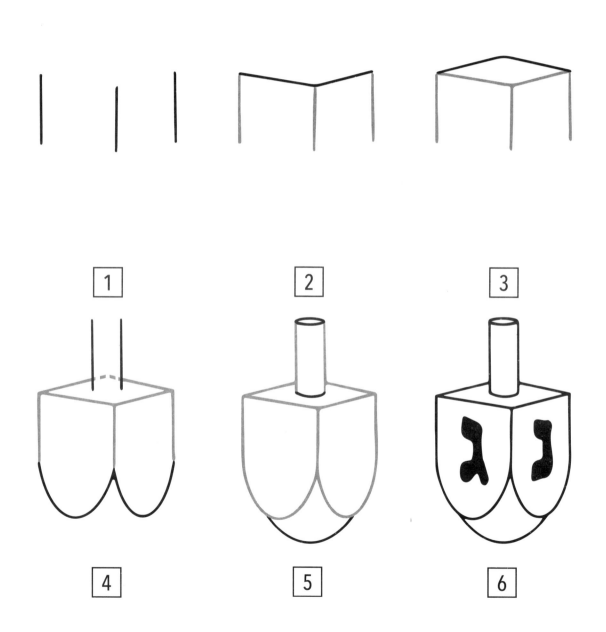

GIFT

The holidays are the perfect time to show your family how much you care for them. Consider gifting your family members some of your amazing new drawings this holiday season!

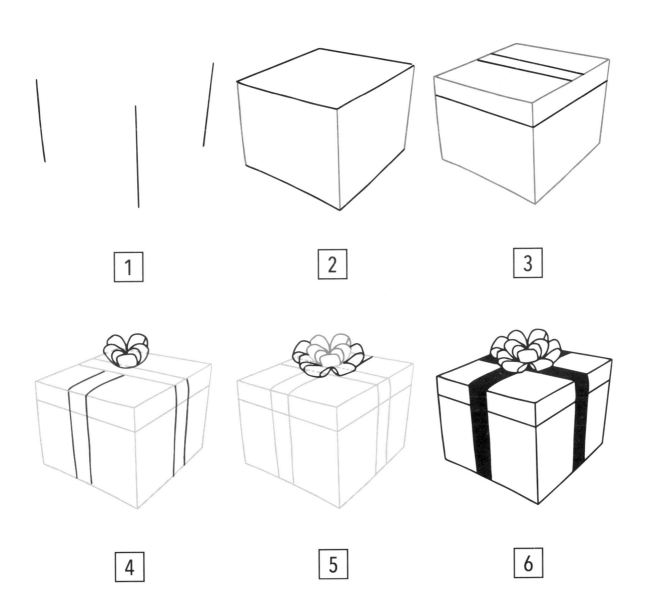

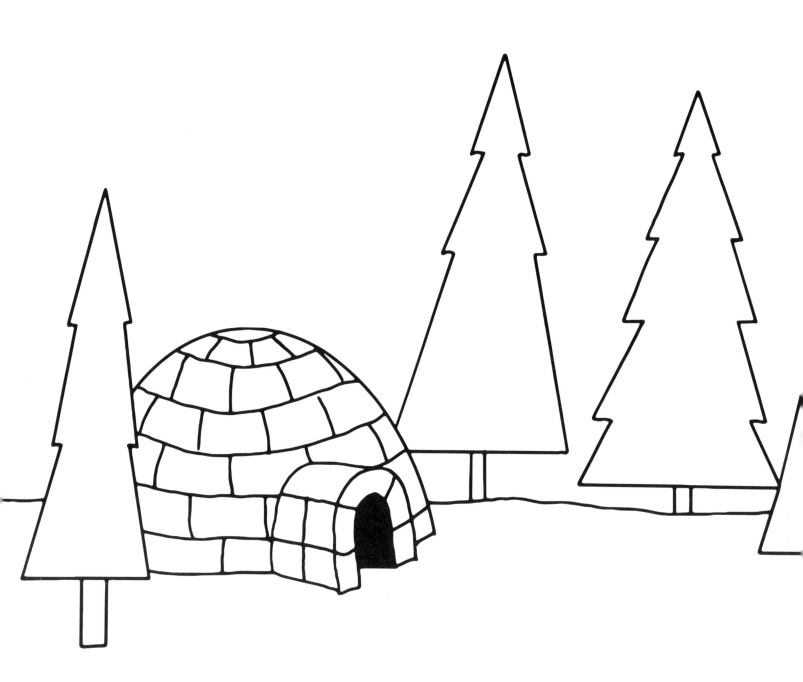

CREATE YOUR OWN

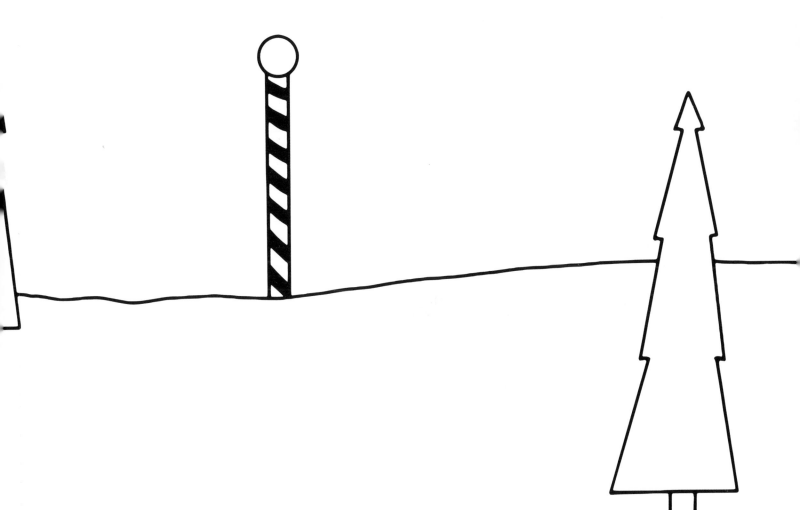

CREATE YOUR OWN GINGERBREAD HOUSE

Use these pages to create a gingerbread house how you would want it!

CREATE YOUR OWN WINTER SCENE

Use these pages to draw your own tree and snowman!

About Alli K

NAME: Alli Koch

HOME: Dallas, Texas

BIRTHDAY: March 20, 1991

FAVORITE COLOR: Black

FAVORITE FOOD: Waffle fries and a large sweet tea

JOB: I am a full-time artist! I sell my art online, paint murals on the sides of buildings, and teach others how to draw or be creative.

WINTER FAVORITE: A warm blanket

PETS: I have one cat named Emmie

CAR: Two-door Jeep

FAMILY: Married to my high school sweetheart

FAVORITE THING TO DO: Play board games!